my
Feather
Signs
Journal

Tracking sacred messages
and meanings
on my life journey

Shanna Lea

Copyright ©2017 by Shanna Lea

Printed in the United States of America

All rights reserved. No part of this book may be reproduced in any form without written permission from the publisher and/or the author/creator at shannalea9@gmail.com

ISBN-13: 978-1545526668
ISBN-10: 1545526664

Dedication

This book is dedicated to all who are seeking answers and following their intuition in doing so.

Feather Signs Journal–Tracking sacred messages and meanings on my life journey

Have you ever seen a feather fall right at your feet? Or find a feather in an odd place, maybe in your house or car where there are no birds or a logical reason for why a feather to be there?

What does it mean?

The question you should be asking is—what does it mean to you?

Were you just thinking of someone special or questioning a change in your life's direction? Or, were you thinking of making a final decision about something and committing to it and a feather suddenly appeared in your path?

Many times feathers appear as a sign from 'the other side' from a loved one you were just thinking about. Or as a confirmation from the spiritual realm, that the thought you just had or a choice you just made is the right one.

Feather Signs

What does it mean when you find a feather? Feathers have been a part of my journey for many years. And I've had many experiences of a feather falling right in front of me just after I've made a decision about something important.

At other times in my life, long stretches of several months or more went by and there were no feather signs that were prominent to me. I followed my intuition and "gut tugs" to tell me if I was still on the right path. I either adjusted my mindset or made a new decision if I had been procrastinating, and then, out of nowhere, a feather appeared. A confirmation on my inner change!

In this journal, I'll give a few facts about feathers and their meanings that are generally understood. But when it comes down to it, the best place for you to learn the meaning is from your own intuition. The gut feeling that tugs you to the answer.

Different cultures all over the world have stories about birds and feathers and their meanings. Aborigines, Native Americans, the Celts, Egyptians—all throughout time these and many other cultures have been closely attuned to nature and the messages it brings. Many of them believed that feathers had several meanings, including new beginnings, rebirth, protection, love and truth.

Today, you can tap into your higher consciousness and pay attention to nature all about you, the same way our ancestors did eons ago, and draw the messages to you like a magnet. You will draw many signs and synchronicities to you energetically. It's a magical experience each time it happens and is like receiving validation, confirmation, or even a 'thumbs up' from the universe that you are on the right track.

What to Write Down

These are some basic questions you can answer in the journal when you find your feather:

• The date when you found the feather
• Where you found the feather
• The color of the feather
• The species of bird it came from
• Your first thoughts, impressions and gut intuitive response to seeing and finding the feather
• What you were thinking or talking about right before the feather appeared
• Or the question or decision you focused on before the feather came to you

Then journal on the second page what this sign means to you. Record your thoughts and what you've learned about this sign or if you have more questions.

To discover a more authentic answer to your questions, fill out this part of your entry first, before you venture online for answers provided by someone else. Someone else's answers may or may not be relevant to your journey.

You will be learning how to tap into your intuition and finding your own answers within. Your intuition is your own Inner Guidance System and is your best guide.

If you've completed the entry and are still unsure about parts of the meaning, then go look up more information. Just remember, you will gain more confidence and connection to the answers by tapping into your intuition first.

I have found that my first initial thoughts and intuition were always much more accurate than meanings looked up on the internet. But sometimes, the meanings found while surfing online, expanded my knowledge of the sign and made my first thoughts more clear.

Along with journaling your first thoughts, you can note the color of the feather, as well as the bird it came from. These meanings can bring clarity to a message that may seem vague at first. You can tap even further into nature by doing a 30 Day Sit Spot to observe birds specifically, and see how the meanings attributed to them are acted out in their daily routines and lives. Many times I've watched a totem animal acting out the very meaning attributed to it and it brought clarification to the symbolism in my own life.

Feather symbolism is connected not only with birds, but other winged creatures as well —dragonflies, butterflies, etc. They are symbols of flight, soaring, freedom, journeys and quests.

Questions to Ask Yourself While Journaling

Asking for a sign

You don't have to just wait around for a feather to fall at your feet. You can ask for a feather sign too! Anytime you want confirmation on something. Be specific: If you have a feeling about something but are second guessing your intuition, then ask for a feather sign. You can ask for it to be a certain color, something rare or unusual. Be prepared to receive it in unexpected ways. If you ask for a very rare or strange color combination, it could come as plastic feathers or a picture on Facebook. You may need to wait and be patient. It can take a few days to a few weeks to appear if you are aligned with your intuition and paying attention to your surroundings.

Is it a sign? How do I know?

Your feather is a sign if it comes to you in an unusual way or place. It will catch your attention. If you believe its a sign, then trust your intuition.

What to Write Down

What does the feather sign mean?

Sometimes the meaning and synchronicity of finding the feather will be obvious to you. You will just know.

But sometimes you may still feel unsure, or that the answer is vague. Give it time, for you are also absorbing it on a subconscious level and the meaning will become clearer as the mud settles in the water. Sometimes other events need to take place before everything clicks and you suddenly understand.

You don't have to understand it immediately. The fun is in the journey through your quest(ions) and discovering the answers as you go.

Just allow the answers to come to you intuitively, don't force them. When you force them, then your brain and ego take over and will lead to wrong assumptions trying to provide an answer. The mind and ego love to be in control and force answers to fit in a certain way, if you let them.

What are the Color Meanings?

Before looking to the internet for color meanings, ask your intuition first what the color means to you. You can journal this more in depth to seek those answers from within yourself.

- What does the color mean to me?
- What do I think of, feel, or remember when I see this color?
- Now look up the universal meanings of the color. Does it align with your first impression or deepen your understanding?

Universal Color Meanings

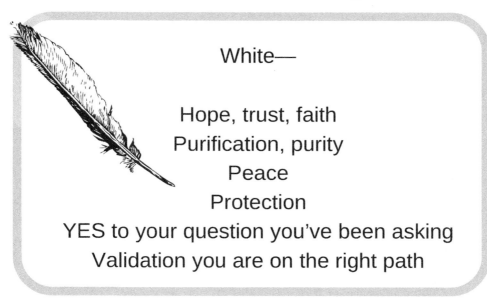

White—

Hope, trust, faith
Purification, purity
Peace
Protection
YES to your question you've been asking
Validation you are on the right path

Red—

Passion
Stability, security
Life force, energy, vitality
Career
Courage
New beginnings, renewal, rebirth

Blue—

Peace, calm, acceptance
Knowledge
Communication, as well as listening
Psychic awareness
Connection with the spirits
Spiritual connection
Healing, cleansing

Yellow—

Joy, cheerfulness, happiness
Mental alertness, staying focused
Vision
Playfulness
New beginnings, renewal, rebirth

Green-

Compassion, forgivness
Health, healing
Vibrant well-being
Growth, abundance, prosperity
Success
Nature, plant spirits, animal spirits, nature spirits
Love, emotions

Orange—

Intimacy, sex, physical relationships
Attraction
Appetite
Staying positive
Creativity, new ideas
Independence
Listening to your inner voice
New beginnings, renewal, rebirth

Pink—

Friendships
Soulmate relationships
Physical creation
Kindness, gentleness
Caring, compassion
Empathy

Purple—

Higher thought
Spiritual connection
Spiritual growth, experiences
Opening of spiritual and psychic sight
Transmute negative energy

Brown—

Earthy
Stability
Grounding
Home life
Balance between physical and spiritual
worlds
Respect
Friendship

Gray—

Wisdom
Mastery
Flexibility
Finding peace within yourself
A neutral position on the issue, not black or white, but in the middle

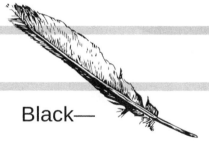

Black—

Death, a chapter closing
Repel negative energy
Spiritual initiation and growth
Wisdom
Magic
Setting boundaries
Confirmation your spirit guides are protecting you

Spotted Colors—

Time to let go of the past
Moving forward

Mixed colors—

Follow your intuition and look back on the individual colors that have meaning for you, and combine the meanings for a deeper understanding of your message. The deeper you listen to your intuition and guidance from within, the more clear the message will be.

What Bird Did My Feather Come From?

Birds, animals and other creatures can all be messengers if you are paying attention to your natural surroundings. Find out what bird the feather came from and learn more about the meaning. Birds and other animals can act as guides, totems and spiritual messengers along your life journey.

For example, I've always used Ted Andrew's book "Animal Speak", in connecting more deeply to animal totems that come to me.

Here are just a few birds and a short reference to their meanings. You can write down a few short words that resonate with you, or do an in-depth study in your journal.

Owl—high wisdom, be aware of your surroundings, signs/omens, meditations will reveal inner wisdom and your answers, prophecy, creative power at night

Sea gull—freedom, seeing things from higher perspective, releasing fear

Crow—change, signs/omens, future event
Sparrow—safety in numbers, community, productivity
Dove—peace, guidance, love and appreciation, nurturing, loved ones in spirit
Duck—speak your truth, stay in the present moment, new opportunities
Mockingbird—power of voice and song, expressing yourself, sacred song, sing your own song
Goose—spiritual awareness, connection to ancestors, good fortune, protection
Eagle—spiritual quest, awakening, opportunities, higher perspective/vision, seeking guidance, freedom,
Hawk—guardianship, far-sightedness, strength
Hummingbird—sweetness of life, swiftness, finding joy in your life, lightness of being

What Do I Do With My Feathers?

If your feathers feel sacred or special to you and you want to keep them, what can you do with them?

• Keep them in a special place, like a decorated shoe box
• Dresser
• Mantle
• Mason jar or vase
• Altar
• Night table beside your bed
• Weave them in a dream catcher
• Put them in the sun visor in your car
• Put in an aquarium with other nature finds such as rocks, shells, pinecones or crystals
• Wooden jewelry box
• In your window
• Press in a book or in the back of this journal
• Or release it back to nature in a special place with thanks of gratitude

How to Use this Journal

In this journal, I've created a place for you to record these magical moments. Take the time to write down your thoughts and impressions to the questions in your journal, and over time you can go back to see the patterns that have unfolded throughout your life's journey.

Have fun on your journey and may you have many feather signs along the way !

In Your Journal:

When you see a feather sign, write down:

• My thoughts right before I saw the feather
• What is going on in my life right now?
• How did I feel when I found the feather?
• What were my first impressions, first feelings and thoughts?
• What does this feather sign mean to me?

Take a few moments to write your thoughts about the encounter, such as the color of the feather, the place you found it, the bird it came from and how those possible meanings play in the overall sign. Then say a word of thanks for the sign.

Feather Signs

Date ___/___/___

Color of feather _____

Bird feather came from _____

My thoughts right before I found the feather

_____
_____
_____
_____
_____

What is going on in my life right now

_____
_____
_____
_____
_____

What are my first impressions? What is my intuition telling me?

_____
_____
_____
_____
_____
_____
_____

My Thoughts & Notes

What does this feather sign mean to me?

Feather Signs

Date ___/___/___

Color of feather _____

Bird feather came from _____

My thoughts right before I found the feather

_____

_____

_____

_____

_____

What is going on in my life right now

_____

_____

_____

_____

_____

What are my first impressions? What is my intuition telling me?

_____

_____

_____

_____

_____

_____

My Thoughts & Notes

What does this feather sign mean to me?

Feather Signs

Date ___/__/__

Color of feather _____

Bird feather came from _____

My thoughts right before I found the feather

_____

_____

_____

_____

_____

What is going on in my life right now

_____

_____

_____

_____

_____

What are my first impressions? What is my
intuition telling me?

_____

_____

_____

_____

_____

_____

_____

My Thoughts & Notes

What does this feather sign mean to me?

Feather Signs

Date ___/___/___

Color of feather _____

Bird feather came from _____

My thoughts right before I found the feather

_____

_____

_____

_____

What is going on in my life right now

_____

_____

_____

_____

What are my first impressions? What is my
intuition telling me?

_____

_____

_____

_____

_____

_____

My Thoughts & Notes

What does this feather sign mean to me?

Feather Signs

Date ___/___/___

Color of feather _____

Bird feather came from _____

My thoughts right before I found the feather

_____

_____

_____

_____

_____

What is going on in my life right now

_____

_____

_____

_____

What are my first impressions? What is my
intuition telling me?

_____

_____

_____

_____

_____

_____

My Thoughts & Notes

What does this feather sign mean to me?

Feather Signs

Date _____/_____/_____

Color of feather _____

Bird feather came from _____

My thoughts right before I found the feather

_____

_____

_____

_____

_____

What is going on in my life right now

_____

_____

_____

_____

_____

What are my first impressions? What is my intuition telling me?

_____

_____

_____

_____

_____

_____

_____

My Thoughts & Notes

What does this feather sign mean to me?

Feather Signs

Date ___/___/___

Color of feather _____

Bird feather came from _____

My thoughts right before I found the feather

_____
_____
_____
_____
_____

What is going on in my life right now

_____
_____
_____
_____
_____

What are my first impressions? What is my intuition telling me?

_____
_____
_____
_____
_____
_____
_____

My Thoughts & Notes

What does this feather sign mean to me?

Feather Signs

Date ___/___/___

Color of feather _____

Bird feather came from _____

My thoughts right before I found the feather

_____

_____

_____

_____

_____

What is going on in my life right now

_____

_____

_____

_____

_____

What are my first impressions? What is my intuition telling me?

_____

_____

_____

_____

_____

_____

_____

My Thoughts & Notes

What does this feather sign mean to me?

Feather Signs

Date ___/___/___

Color of feather _____

Bird feather came from _____

My thoughts right before I found the feather

_____

_____

_____

_____

_____

What is going on in my life right now

_____

_____

_____

_____

_____

What are my first impressions? What is my
intuition telling me?

_____

_____

_____

_____

_____

_____

My Thoughts & Notes

What does this feather sign mean to me?

Feather Signs

Date ___/___/___

Color of feather _____

Bird feather came from _____

My thoughts right before I found the feather

_____

_____

_____

_____

What is going on in my life right now

_____

_____

_____

_____

What are my first impressions? What is my intuition telling me?

_____

_____

_____

_____

_____

_____

My Thoughts & Notes

What does this feather sign mean to me?

Feather Signs

Date ___/___/___

Color of feather _____

Bird feather came from _____

My thoughts right before I found the feather

_____

_____

_____

_____

What is going on in my life right now

_____

_____

_____

_____

What are my first impressions? What is my intuition telling me?

_____

_____

_____

_____

_____

_____

My Thoughts & Notes

What does this feather sign mean to me?

Feather Signs

Date ___/___/___

Color of feather _____

Bird feather came from _____

My thoughts right before I found the feather

_____

_____

_____

_____

_____

What is going on in my life right now

_____

_____

_____

_____

_____

What are my first impressions? What is my intuition telling me?

_____

_____

_____

_____

_____

_____

_____

My Thoughts & Notes

What does this feather sign mean to me?

Feather Signs

Date   ___/___/___

Color of feather   _____

Bird feather came from   _____

My thoughts right before I found the feather

_____

_____

_____

_____

_____

What is going on in my life right now

_____

_____

_____

_____

_____

What are my first impressions? What is my intuition telling me?

_____

_____

_____

_____

_____

_____

_____

My Thoughts & Notes

What does this feather sign mean to me?

Feather Signs

Date ___/___/___

Color of feather _____

Bird feather came from _____

My thoughts right before I found the feather

_____

_____

_____

_____

_____

What is going on in my life right now

_____

_____

_____

_____

_____

What are my first impressions? What is my intuition telling me?

_____

_____

_____

_____

_____

_____

_____

My Thoughts & Notes

What does this feather sign mean to me?

Feather Signs

Date ___/___/___

Color of feather _____

Bird feather came from _____

My thoughts right before I found the feather

_____

_____

_____

_____

_____

What is going on in my life right now

_____

_____

_____

_____

_____

What are my first impressions? What is my
intuition telling me?

_____

_____

_____

_____

_____

_____

My Thoughts & Notes

What does this feather sign mean to me?

Feather Signs

Date ___/__/__

Color of feather _____

Bird feather came from _____

My thoughts right before I found the feather

_____

_____

_____

_____

_____

What is going on in my life right now

_____

_____

_____

_____

What are my first impressions? What is my intuition telling me?

_____

_____

_____

_____

_____

_____

My Thoughts & Notes

What does this feather sign mean to me?

Feather Signs

Date ___/___/___

Color of feather _____

Bird feather came from _____

My thoughts right before I found the feather

_____
_____
_____
_____
_____

What is going on in my life right now

_____
_____
_____
_____
_____

What are my first impressions? What is my intuition telling me?

_____
_____
_____
_____
_____
_____
_____

My Thoughts & Notes

What does this feather sign mean to me?

Feather Signs

Date ___/___/___

Color of feather _____

Bird feather came from _____

My thoughts right before I found the feather

_____
_____
_____
_____
_____

What is going on in my life right now

_____
_____
_____
_____
_____

What are my first impressions? What is my
intuition telling me?

_____
_____
_____
_____
_____
_____
_____

My Thoughts & Notes

What does this feather sign mean to me?

Feather Signs

Date ___/___/___

Color of feather _____

Bird feather came from _____

My thoughts right before I found the feather

_____

_____

_____

_____

_____

What is going on in my life right now

_____

_____

_____

_____

_____

What are my first impressions? What is my intuition telling me?

_____

_____

_____

_____

_____

_____

_____

My Thoughts & Notes

What does this feather sign mean to me?

Feather Signs

Date ___/___/___

Color of feather _____

Bird feather came from _____

My thoughts right before I found the feather

_____

_____

_____

_____

_____

What is going on in my life right now

_____

_____

_____

_____

_____

What are my first impressions? What is my intuition telling me?

_____

_____

_____

_____

_____

_____

_____

My Thoughts & Notes

What does this feather sign mean to me?

Feather Signs

Date ___/___/___

Color of feather _____

Bird feather came from _____

My thoughts right before I found the feather

_____

_____

_____

_____

_____

What is going on in my life right now

_____

_____

_____

_____

_____

What are my first impressions? What is my intuition telling me?

_____

_____

_____

_____

_____

_____

My Thoughts & Notes

What does this feather sign mean to me?

Feather Signs

Date ___/___/___

Color of feather _____

Bird feather came from _____

My thoughts right before I found the feather

_____
_____
_____
_____
_____

What is going on in my life right now

_____
_____
_____
_____
_____

What are my first impressions? What is my intuition telling me?

_____
_____
_____
_____
_____
_____
_____

My Thoughts & Notes

What does this feather sign mean to me?

Feather Signs

Date ___/___/___

Color of feather _____

Bird feather came from _____

My thoughts right before I found the feather

_____

_____

_____

_____

_____

What is going on in my life right now

_____

_____

_____

_____

_____

What are my first impressions? What is my intuition telling me?

_____

_____

_____

_____

_____

_____

_____

My Thoughts & Notes

What does this feather sign mean to me?

Feather Signs

Date ___/___/___

Color of feather _____

Bird feather came from _____

My thoughts right before I found the feather

_____

_____

_____

_____

_____

What is going on in my life right now

_____

_____

_____

_____

_____

What are my first impressions? What is my
intuition telling me?

_____

_____

_____

_____

_____

_____

My Thoughts & Notes

What does this feather sign mean to me?

Feather Signs

Date ___/___/___

Color of feather _____

Bird feather came from _____

My thoughts right before I found the feather

_____
_____
_____
_____
_____

What is going on in my life right now

_____
_____
_____
_____
_____

What are my first impressions? What is my intuition telling me?

_____
_____
_____
_____
_____
_____
_____

My Thoughts & Notes

What does this feather sign mean to me?

Feather Signs

Date ___/___/___

Color of feather _____

Bird feather came from _____

My thoughts right before I found the feather

_____

_____

_____

_____

_____

What is going on in my life right now

_____

_____

_____

_____

_____

What are my first impressions? What is my intuition telling me?

_____

_____

_____

_____

_____

_____

My Thoughts & Notes

What does this feather sign mean to me?

Feather Signs

Date ___/___/___

Color of feather _____

Bird feather came from _____

My thoughts right before I found the feather

_____

_____

_____

_____

_____

What is going on in my life right now

_____

_____

_____

_____

What are my first impressions? What is my intuition telling me?

_____

_____

_____

_____

_____

_____

My Thoughts & Notes

What does this feather sign mean to me?

Feather Signs

Date ___/___/___

Color of feather _____

Bird feather came from _____

My thoughts right before I found the feather

_____

_____

_____

_____

_____

What is going on in my life right now

_____

_____

_____

_____

_____

What are my first impressions? What is my
intuition telling me?

_____

_____

_____

_____

_____

_____

My Thoughts & Notes

What does this feather sign mean to me?

Feather Signs

Date ___/___/___

Color of feather _____

Bird feather came from _____

My thoughts right before I found the feather

_____

_____

_____

_____

_____

What is going on in my life right now

_____

_____

_____

_____

_____

What are my first impressions? What is my
intuition telling me?

_____

_____

_____

_____

_____

_____

My Thoughts & Notes

What does this feather sign mean to me?

Feather Signs

Date ___/__/__

Color of feather _____

Bird feather came from _____

My thoughts right before I found the feather

_____

_____

_____

_____

_____

What is going on in my life right now

_____

_____

_____

_____

What are my first impressions? What is my intuition telling me?

_____

_____

_____

_____

_____

_____

My Thoughts & Notes

What does this feather sign mean to me?

Feather Signs

Date ___/___/___

Color of feather _____

Bird feather came from _____

My thoughts right before I found the feather

_____

_____

_____

_____

_____

What is going on in my life right now

_____

_____

_____

_____

_____

What are my first impressions? What is my
intuition telling me?

_____

_____

_____

_____

_____

_____

_____

My Thoughts & Notes

What does this feather sign mean to me?

Feather Signs

Date ___/___/___

Color of feather _____

Bird feather came from _____

My thoughts right before I found the feather

_____
_____
_____
_____
_____

What is going on in my life right now

_____
_____
_____
_____
_____

What are my first impressions? What is my
intuition telling me?

_____
_____
_____
_____
_____
_____
_____

My Thoughts & Notes

What does this feather sign mean to me?

Feather Signs

Date ___/___/___

Color of feather _____

Bird feather came from _____

My thoughts right before I found the feather

_____

_____

_____

_____

_____

What is going on in my life right now

_____

_____

_____

_____

_____

What are my first impressions? What is my intuition telling me?

_____

_____

_____

_____

_____

_____

My Thoughts & Notes

What does this feather sign mean to me?

Feather Signs

Date ___/___/___

Color of feather _____

Bird feather came from _____

My thoughts right before I found the feather

_____

_____

_____

_____

_____

What is going on in my life right now

_____

_____

_____

_____

What are my first impressions? What is my intuition telling me?

_____

_____

_____

_____

_____

_____

My Thoughts & Notes

What does this feather sign mean to me?

Feather Signs

Date ___/___/___

Color of feather _____

Bird feather came from _____

My thoughts right before I found the feather

_____
_____
_____
_____
_____

What is going on in my life right now

_____
_____
_____
_____
_____

What are my first impressions? What is my intuition telling me?

_____
_____
_____
_____
_____
_____
_____

My Thoughts & Notes

What does this feather sign mean to me?

Feather Signs

Date ___/___/___

Color of feather _____

Bird feather came from _____

My thoughts right before I found the feather

_____

_____

_____

_____

_____

What is going on in my life right now

_____

_____

_____

_____

_____

What are my first impressions? What is my intuition telling me?

_____

_____

_____

_____

_____

_____

My Thoughts & Notes

What does this feather sign mean to me?

Feather Signs

Date ___/___/___

Color of feather _____

Bird feather came from _____

My thoughts right before I found the feather

_____

_____

_____

_____

_____

What is going on in my life right now

_____

_____

_____

_____

_____

What are my first impressions? What is my intuition telling me?

_____

_____

_____

_____

_____

_____

_____

My Thoughts & Notes

What does this feather sign mean to me?

Feather Signs

Date ___/___/___

Color of feather _____

Bird feather came from _____

My thoughts right before I found the feather

_____

_____

_____

_____

_____

What is going on in my life right now

_____

_____

_____

_____

_____

What are my first impressions? What is my
intuition telling me?

_____

_____

_____

_____

_____

_____

_____

My Thoughts & Notes

What does this feather sign mean to me?

Feather Signs

Date ___/___/___

Color of feather _____

Bird feather came from _____

My thoughts right before I found the feather

_____

_____

_____

_____

_____

What is going on in my life right now

_____

_____

_____

_____

What are my first impressions? What is my intuition telling me?

_____

_____

_____

_____

_____

_____

My Thoughts & Notes

What does this feather sign mean to me?

Feather Signs

Date ___/___/__

Color of feather _____

Bird feather came from _____

My thoughts right before I found the feather

_____

_____

_____

_____

_____

What is going on in my life right now

_____

_____

_____

_____

_____

What are my first impressions? What is my intuition telling me?

_____

_____

_____

_____

_____

_____

My Thoughts & Notes

What does this feather sign mean to me?

Feather Signs

Date ___/___/___

Color of feather _____

Bird feather came from _____

My thoughts right before I found the feather

_____

_____

_____

_____

_____

What is going on in my life right now

_____

_____

_____

_____

What are my first impressions? What is my intuition telling me?

_____

_____

_____

_____

_____

_____

My Thoughts & Notes

What does this feather sign mean to me?

Feather Signs

Date ___/___/___

Color of feather _____

Bird feather came from _____

My thoughts right before I found the feather

_____

_____

_____

_____

_____

What is going on in my life right now

_____

_____

_____

_____

_____

What are my first impressions? What is my intuition telling me?

_____

_____

_____

_____

_____

_____

_____

My Thoughts & Notes

What does this feather sign mean to me?

Feather Signs

Date ___/___/___

Color of feather _____

Bird feather came from _____

My thoughts right before I found the feather

_____

_____

_____

_____

_____

What is going on in my life right now

_____

_____

_____

_____

_____

What are my first impressions? What is my intuition telling me?

_____

_____

_____

_____

_____

_____

My Thoughts & Notes

What does this feather sign mean to me?

Feather Signs

Date ___/___/___

Color of feather _____

Bird feather came from _____

My thoughts right before I found the feather

_____

_____

_____

_____

_____

What is going on in my life right now

_____

_____

_____

_____

_____

What are my first impressions? What is my
intuition telling me?

_____

_____

_____

_____

_____

_____

_____

My Thoughts & Notes

What does this feather sign mean to me?

Feather Signs

Date ___/___/___

Color of feather _____

Bird feather came from _____

My thoughts right before I found the feather

_____

_____

_____

_____

_____

What is going on in my life right now

_____

_____

_____

_____

What are my first impressions? What is my intuition telling me?

_____

_____

_____

_____

_____

My Thoughts & Notes

What does this feather sign mean to me?

Feather Signs

Date ___/___/__

Color of feather _____

Bird feather came from _____

My thoughts right before I found the feather

_____
_____
_____
_____

What is going on in my life right now

_____
_____
_____
_____

What are my first impressions? What is my intuition telling me?

_____
_____
_____
_____
_____

My Thoughts & Notes

What does this feather sign mean to me?

Feather Signs

Date ___/___/___

Color of feather _____

Bird feather came from _____

My thoughts right before I found the feather

_____

_____

_____

_____

_____

What is going on in my life right now

_____

_____

_____

_____

What are my first impressions? What is my intuition telling me?

_____

_____

_____

_____

_____

_____

My Thoughts & Notes

What does this feather sign mean to me?

Feather Signs

Date ___/__/__

Color of feather _____

Bird feather came from _____

My thoughts right before I found the feather

_____

_____

_____

_____

_____

What is going on in my life right now

_____

_____

_____

_____

What are my first impressions? What is my
intuition telling me?

_____

_____

_____

_____

_____

_____

My Thoughts & Notes

What does this feather sign mean to me?

Feather Signs

Date ___/___/___

Color of feather _____

Bird feather came from _____

My thoughts right before I found the feather

_____

_____

_____

_____

_____

What is going on in my life right now

_____

_____

_____

_____

What are my first impressions? What is my intuition telling me?

_____

_____

_____

_____

_____

_____

My Thoughts & Notes

What does this feather sign mean to me?

Feather Signs

Date ___/___/___

Color of feather _____

Bird feather came from _____

My thoughts right before I found the feather

_____

_____

_____

_____

What is going on in my life right now

_____

_____

_____

_____

What are my first impressions? What is my intuition telling me?

_____

_____

_____

_____

_____

_____

My Thoughts & Notes

What does this feather sign mean to me?

Feather Signs

Date ___/___/___

Color of feather _____

Bird feather came from _____

My thoughts right before I found the feather

_____

_____

_____

_____

_____

What is going on in my life right now

_____

_____

_____

_____

_____

What are my first impressions? What is my intuition telling me?

_____

_____

_____

_____

_____

_____

My Thoughts & Notes

What does this feather sign mean to me?

Feather Signs

Date ___/___/___

Color of feather _____

Bird feather came from _____

My thoughts right before I found the feather

_____

_____

_____

_____

_____

What is going on in my life right now

_____

_____

_____

_____

_____

What are my first impressions? What is my intuition telling me?

_____

_____

_____

_____

_____

_____

_____

My Thoughts & Notes

What does this feather sign mean to me?

Feather Signs

Date ___/___/___

Color of feather _____

Bird feather came from _____

My thoughts right before I found the feather

_____

_____

_____

_____

What is going on in my life right now

_____

_____

_____

_____

What are my first impressions? What is my intuition telling me?

_____

_____

_____

_____

_____

My Thoughts & Notes

What does this feather sign mean to me?

Feather Signs

Date ___/___/___

Color of feather _____

Bird feather came from _____

My thoughts right before I found the feather

_____

_____

_____

_____

What is going on in my life right now

_____

_____

_____

_____

What are my first impressions? What is my intuition telling me?

_____

_____

_____

_____

_____

_____

My Thoughts & Notes

What does this feather sign mean to me?

Feather Signs

Date ___/___/___

Color of feather _____

Bird feather came from _____

My thoughts right before I found the feather

_____
_____
_____
_____
_____

What is going on in my life right now

_____
_____
_____
_____

What are my first impressions? What is my intuition telling me?

_____
_____
_____
_____
_____
_____

My Thoughts & Notes

What does this feather sign mean to me?

Feather Signs

Date ___/___/___

Color of feather _____

Bird feather came from _____

My thoughts right before I found the feather

_____

_____

_____

_____

What is going on in my life right now

_____

_____

_____

_____

What are my first impressions? What is my intuition telling me?

_____

_____

_____

_____

_____

_____

My Thoughts & Notes

What does this feather sign mean to me?

Feather Signs

Date ___/___/___

Color of feather _____

Bird feather came from _____

My thoughts right before I found the feather

_____

_____

_____

_____

_____

What is going on in my life right now

_____

_____

_____

_____

_____

What are my first impressions? What is my intuition telling me?

_____

_____

_____

_____

_____

_____

My Thoughts & Notes

What does this feather sign mean to me?

Feather Signs

Date ___/__/__

Color of feather _____

Bird feather came from _____

My thoughts right before I found the feather

_____

_____

_____

_____

What is going on in my life right now

_____

_____

_____

_____

What are my first impressions? What is my intuition telling me?

_____

_____

_____

_____

_____

_____

My Thoughts & Notes

What does this feather sign mean to me?

Feather Signs

Date ___/__/__

Color of feather _____

Bird feather came from _____

My thoughts right before I found the feather

_____

_____

_____

_____

_____

What is going on in my life right now

_____

_____

_____

_____

_____

What are my first impressions? What is my
intuition telling me?

_____

_____

_____

_____

_____

_____

My Thoughts & Notes

What does this feather sign mean to me?

Feather Signs

Date ___/___/___

Color of feather _____

Bird feather came from _____

My thoughts right before I found the feather

_____

_____

_____

_____

_____

What is going on in my life right now

_____

_____

_____

_____

_____

What are my first impressions? What is my
intuition telling me?

_____

_____

_____

_____

_____

_____

My Thoughts & Notes

What does this feather sign mean to me?

My Found Feathers

Tape or glue your feathers on these pages. Write a short note with each one and the date you wrote about it in your journal.

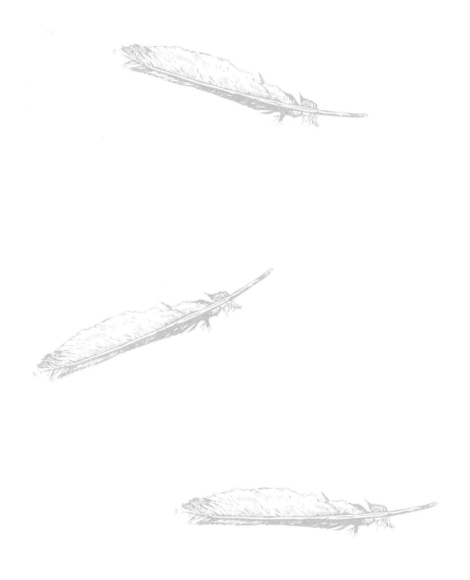

My Found Feathers

Tape or glue your feathers on these pages. Write a short note with each one and the date you wrote about it in your journal.

My Found Feathers

Tape or glue your feathers on these pages. Write a short note with each one and the date you wrote about it in your journal.

My Found Feathers

Tape or glue your feathers on these pages. Write a short note with each one and the date you wrote about it in your journal.

My Found Feathers

Tape or glue your feathers on these pages. Write a short note with each one and the date you wrote about it in your journal.

My Found Feathers

Tape or glue your feathers on these pages. Write a short note with each one and the date you wrote about it in your journal.

My Found Feathers

Tape or glue your feathers on these pages. Write a short note with each one and the date you wrote about it in your journal.

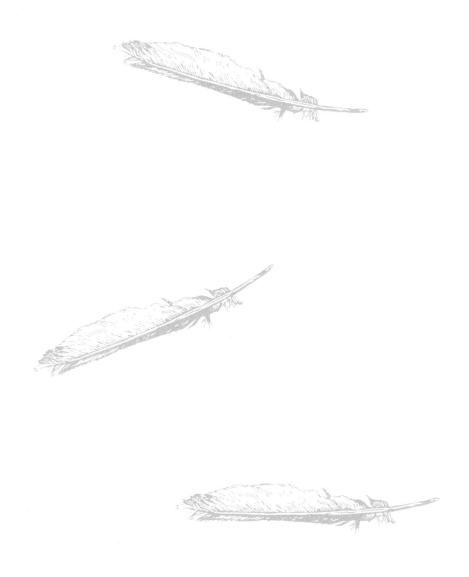

My Found Feathers

Tape or glue your feathers on these pages. Write a short note with each one and the date you wrote about it in your journal.

My Found Feathers

Tape or glue your feathers on these pages. Write a short note with each one and the date you wrote about it in your journal.

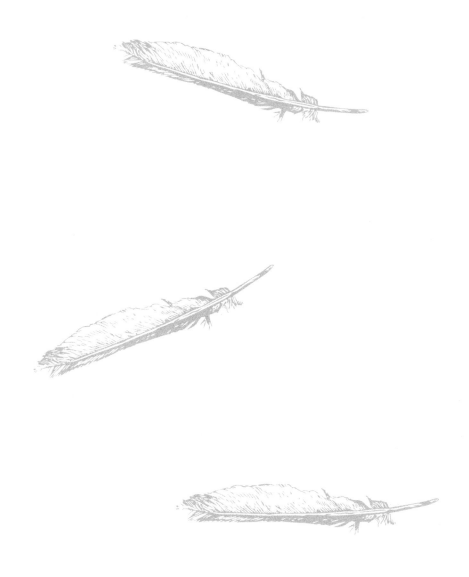

My Found Feathers

Tape or glue your feathers on these pages. Write a short note with each one and the date you wrote about it in your journal.

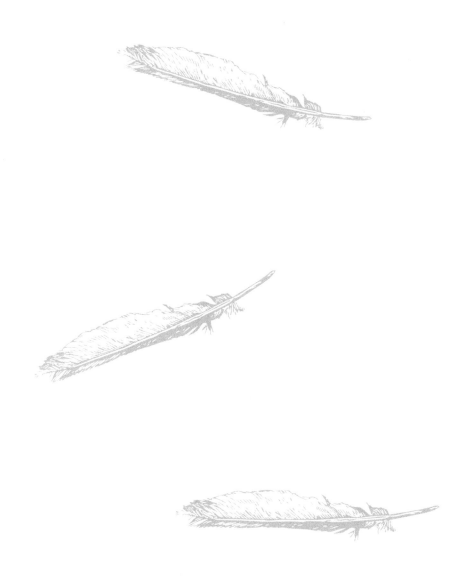

My Found Feathers

Tape or glue your feathers on these pages. Write a short note with each one and the date you wrote about it in your journal.

My Found Feathers

Tape or glue your feathers on these pages. Write a short note with each one and the date you wrote about it in your journal.

My Found Feathers

Tape or glue your feathers on these pages. Write a short note with each one and the date you wrote about it in your journal.

My Found Feathers

Tape or glue your feathers on these pages. Write a short note with each one and the date you wrote about it in your journal.

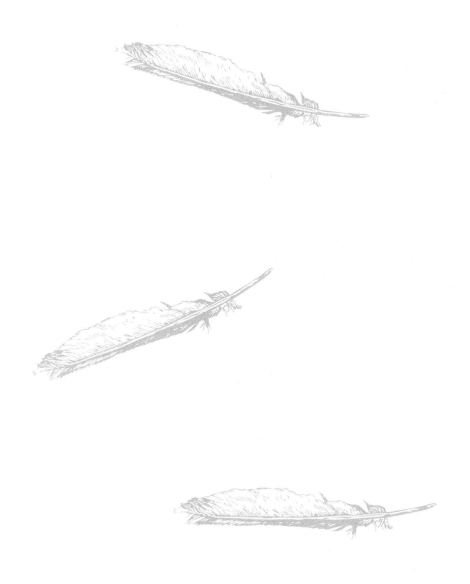

My Found Feathers

Tape or glue your feathers on these pages. Write a short note with each one and the date you wrote about it in your journal.

My Found Feathers

Tape or glue your feathers on these pages. Write a short note with each one and the date you wrote about it in your journal.

My Found Feathers

Tape or glue your feathers on these pages. Write a short note with each one and the date you wrote about it in your journal.

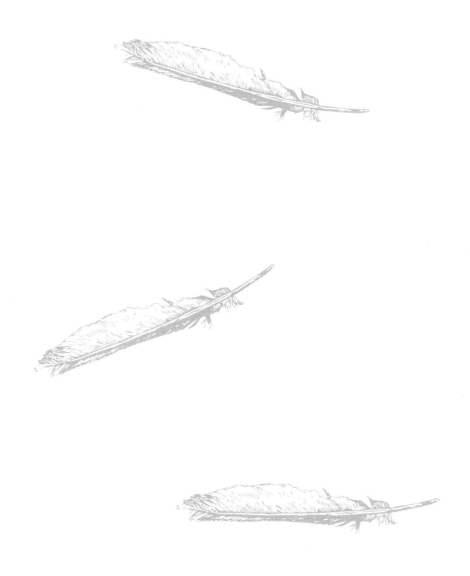

My Found Feathers

Tape or glue your feathers on these pages. Write a short note with each one and the date you wrote about it in your journal.

My Found Feathers

Tape or glue your feathers on these pages. Write a short note with each one and the date you wrote about it in your journal.

My Found Feathers

Tape or glue your feathers on these pages. Write a short note with each one and the date you wrote about it in your journal.

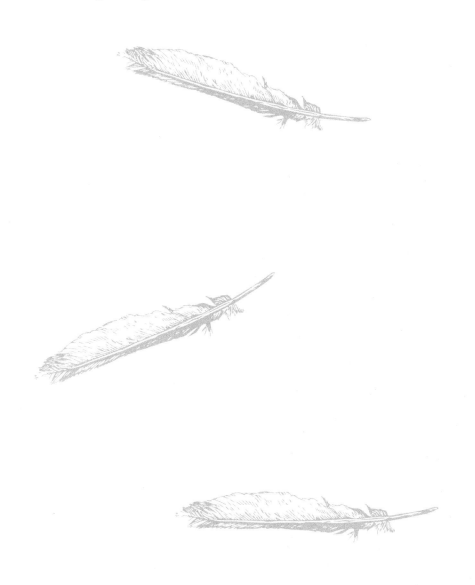

My Found Feathers

Tape or glue your feathers on these pages. Write a short note with each one and the date you wrote about it in your journal.

My Found Feathers

Tape or glue your feathers on these pages. Write a short note with each one and the date you wrote about it in your journal.

My Found Feathers

Tape or glue your feathers on these pages. Write a short note with each one and the date you wrote about it in your journal.

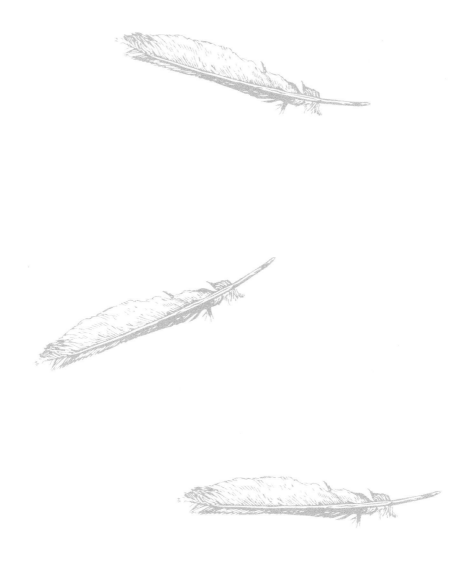

My Found Feathers

Tape or glue your feathers on these pages. Write a short note with each one and the date you wrote about it in your journal.

My Found Feathers

Tape or glue your feathers on these pages. Write a short note with each one and the date you wrote about it in your journal.

My Found Feathers

Tape or glue your feathers on these pages. Write a short note with each one and the date you wrote about it in your journal.

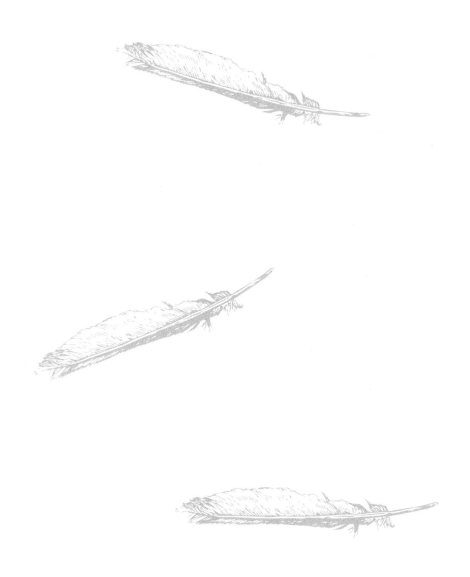

My Found Feathers

Tape or glue your feathers on these pages. Write a short note with each one and the date you wrote about it in your journal.

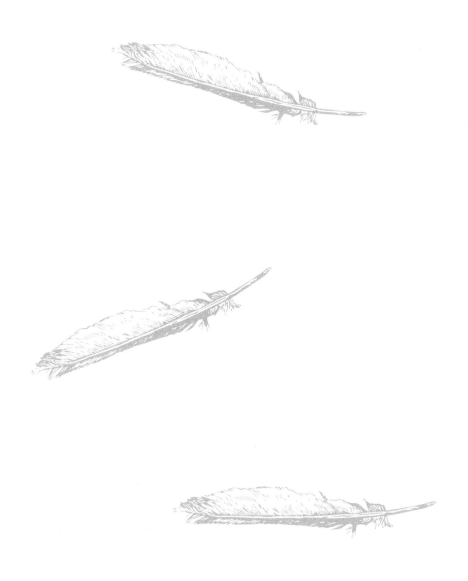

My Found Feathers

Tape or glue your feathers on these pages. Write a short note with each one and the date you wrote about it in your journal.

My Found Feathers

Tape or glue your feathers on these pages. Write a short note with each one and the date you wrote about it in your journal.

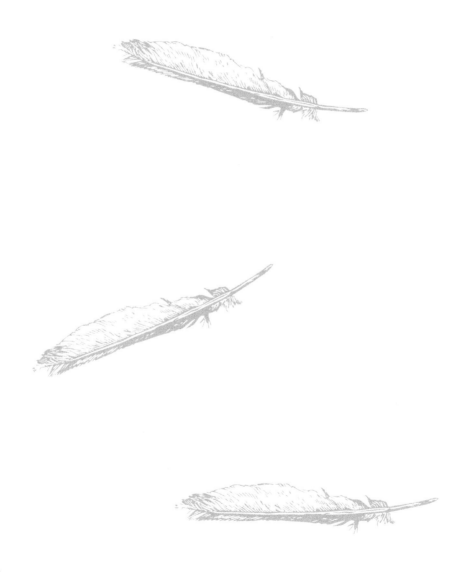

My Found Feathers

Tape or glue your feathers on these pages. Write a short note with each one and the date you wrote about it in your journal.

Printed in Great Britain
by Amazon